BADASS BEST QUOTES

kinkajou

Breaking Bad

Badass Best Quotes
Published by Kinkajou
Copyright © Frances Lincoln Limited 2015

A catalogue record for this book is available
from the British Library

Designed by Sarah Allberrey

Background Texture © arigato/Shutterstock.com
Film Strip Illustration © Nasared/Shutterstock.com

Kinkajou is an imprint of Frances Lincoln Limited
74–77 White Lion Street
London N1 9PF
www.kinkajou.com

ISBN: 978-0-7112-3688-2
Printed in China

10 9 8 7 6 5 4 3 2 1

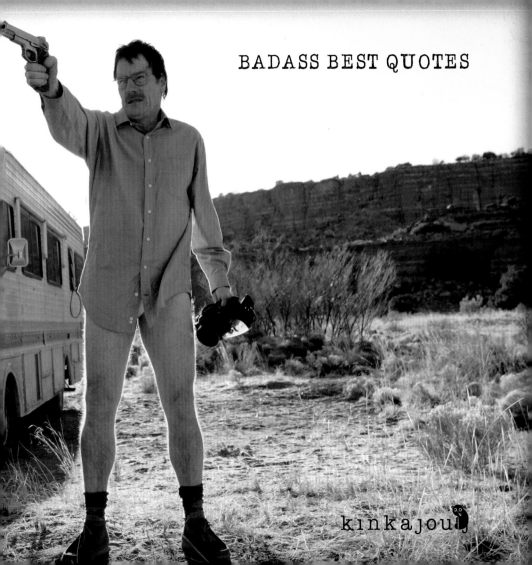

BADASS BEST QUOTES

kinkajou

SEASON 1

[EP.1]

> **WALT**
> Did you learn nothing from my
> chemistry class?

> **JESSE**
> No, you flunked me, remember?

> **JESSE**
> Nah, come on man. Some straight like you,
> giant stick up his ass and all a sudden at
> age, what, 60, he's just gonna break bad?

> **WALT**
> Look, we are in this fifty-fifty. Okay?

[EP.3]

> **KRAZY-8**
> Walter, I don't know what you think
> you're doing here, but trust me, this line
> of work doesn't suit you.

> HANK
> So be on notice. We got new players in town.
> We don't know who they are, where they come
> from . . . but they possess an extremely high skill
> set. Me personally? I'm thinking Albuquerque just
> might have a new kingpin.

> WALT
> I have cancer, lung cancer. It's bad.

> JESSE
> Well, it's just basic chemistry, yo.

> JESSE
> You may know a lot about chemistry, man, but
> you don't know jack about slinging dope.

> TUCO
> Boo-yah! Whoo! Haha! This kicks like a mule with
> his balls wrapped in duct tape.

[EP.6]

> **TUCO**
> Sometimes you gotta rob to keep
> your riches.

[EP.7]

> **JESSE**
> So you do have a plan. Yeah,
> Mr. White! Yeah, science!

> **JESSE**
> How much cash do you need?
>
> **WALT**
> More.

> **TUCO**
> Oh, blue, yellow, pink. Whatever,
> man. Just keep bringing me that.

NAME: WALTER HARTWELL WHITE

AKA: WALT, MR. WHITE, HEISENBERG

When Walter White, a dutiful husband,
father, and high school chemistry
teacher, is diagnosed with inoperable
lung cancer, he begins to cook crystal
methamphetamine in order to pay his
medical bills and to put by enough cash
for his family to live on when he is gone.
Being both a brilliant chemist and a
perfectionist, Walt comes up with the
purest product ever to hit the streets –
and because it's blue, the most distinctive.
Walt starts out abhorring violence, but soon
comes to realise that it is a necessary evil in
his new line of work. As he becomes more
deeply embroiled in the world of drugs,
he develops a ruthless personality, often
letting his ego get the better of him. The one
thing that remains constant is his sense
of responsibility to his wife and family.

"Chemistry is the study of
matter. But I prefer to see
it as the study of change.
Now just think about this.
Electrons. They change their
energy levels. Molecules.
Molecules change their bonds.
Elements. They combine
and change into compounds.
Well, that's all of life. Right?
I mean, it's just the constant.
It's the cycle. It's solution,
dissolution, just over and over
and over. It is growth, then
decay, then transformation.
It is fascinating, really."
– Walter White

SEASON 2

[EP.1]

> SKYLER
>
> New hat?

> WALT
>
> Yeah.

[EP.4]

> JESSE
>
> I just need my half of the money, and
> I will go.

> WALT
>
> Your half? There is no your half of the money.
> There is only my all of it. Do you understand?

[EP.5]

> HANK
>
> Well, we keep hearing a name. Heisenberg.
> Lately pretty much every dime-bagger we
> come across.

> ASAC
>
> Heisenberg?

> HANK
>
> Yeah, I know. Maybe it's a tweaker urban
> legend. Still, somebody somewhere is cooking
> that big blue we keep finding.

[EP.5]

> **MARIE**
> So let me get this straight. You call in
> sick the day after receiving a long-awaited,
> career-boosting promotion, so you can
> play Oktoberfest in your man cave?

[EP.6]

> **SKINNY PETE**
> Hey, man. I'm slinging mad volume and
> fat stacking Benjies, you know what I'm
> saying? I can't be all about, like spelling,
> and shit.

[EP.7]

> **JESSE**
> I'm a blowfish. Yeah! Blow fishing this up.

> **JESSE**
> Now, we're gonna be kings, understand.
> Well, I'm gonna be king, you guys will be
> princes or dukes or something.

> **BADGER**
> I wanna be a knight.

"The thing is, if you
just do stuff, and
nothing happens,
what's it all mean?
What's the point?"
– Jesse Pinkman

NAME: JESSE BRUCE PINKMAN
AKA: JESSE JACKSON, CAP'N COOK

Chilli powder was Jesse's trademark ingredient when he cooked his own meth as small-time operator, Cap'n Cook. When his old chemistry teacher, Mr. White, approached him for help Jesse was more than a little surprised. Walt teaches Jesse how to cook meth of a higher standard, albeit without the chilli, and begins to observe his ex-student with a combination of exasperation and pride. As Walt develops fatherly feelings towards him, Jesse's loyalty to Walt builds - although he never can bring himself to call Walt anything other then Mr. White. Jesse eventually becomes an excellent cook with results almost as pure as his teacher's. As Jesse's wealth accumulates, money becomes meaningless to him in the face of terrible loss.

                    JESSE
        Seriously, when the going gets tough,
        you don't want a criminal lawyer.
        You want a "criminal" lawyer.

        _____

                    SAUL
        So if you wanna make more money
        and, uh, keep the money you make
        . . . better call Saul!

        _____

                    JESSE
        Us. All right? I'm talking about us.

                    JANE
        Us.

                    JESSE
        Yeah. You and me.

                    JANE
        Who's you and me?

        _____

                    WALT
        Stay out of my territory.

[EP.11]

SKINNY PETE
This game we playing? We don't have the
street cred to survive it.

SAUL
You two suck at peddling meth. Period.

SAUL
Let's just say I know a guy who knows a
guy. Who knows another guy.

[EP.12]

WALT
If I tell you the truth, will you stay?
Stay, and I will tell you everything.

SKYLER
Whatever it is, I'm afraid to know.

SEASON 3

[EP.1]

                    JESSE
It's all about accepting who you really are.
I accept who I am.

                    WALT
And who are you?

                    JESSE
I'm the bad guy.

[EP.2]

                    SAUL
Talent like that and he flushes it down the
crapper. It's like Michelangelo won't paint.

[EP.3]

                    WALT
This family is everything to me. Without it,
I have nothing to lose.

                    WALT
Honesty is good. Don't you think?

                    SKYLER
I fucked Ted.

[EP.4]

MIKE

You know, Walter, sometimes it doesn't hurt to have someone watching your back.

_____

WALT JR.

These eggs are good, Mom.

_____

[EP.5]

WALT

The chemistry must be respected.

_____

MARIE

Facing death, it changes a person. It has to, don't you think?

_____

GUS

What does a man do, Walter? A man provides for his family.

NAME: SKYLER WHITE (née Lambert)

Skyler is pregnant when she learns that her
husband, Walt, has been diagnosed with lung
cancer. Already deeply worried about his
health, Skyler becomes increasingly puzzled
and alarmed by his odd behaviour as Walt
does his best to hide his new lifestyle from
her. When she eventually discovers the truth
about Walt's new business, she flees to her
sister's house taking Walt Junior and baby
Holly with her. Wanting her family back
together again, Skyler eventually relents
and joins Walt, helping to launder the drug
money by running the A1A Carwash, a
business they acquire for that very purpose.

Although Skyler loves Walt, she becomes ever
more frightened and concerned for the safety
of her children and puts their well being first.

"We have discussed
everything we
need to discuss...
I thought I made
myself clear."
– Skyler White

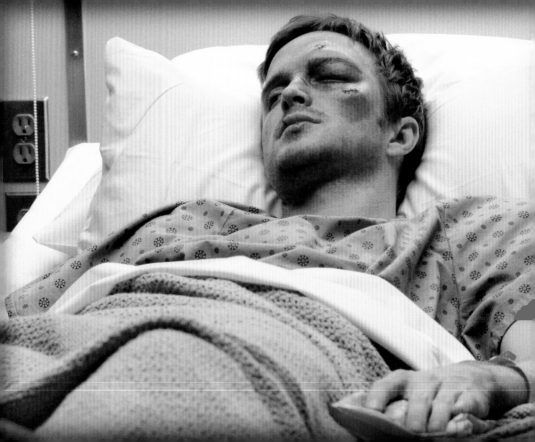

[EP.6]

SKINNY PETE

Heisenberg who? That's what I say. My man
Jesse can cook. Check it, yo. It ain't cloudy or
dirty or nothing. Just the right shade of blue.

GALE

I love the lab. Because it's all still magic.
You know?

JESSE

This is my own private domicile and I will not be
harassed. Bitch.

[EP.7]

SAUL
(TO JESSE IN HOSPITAL)
Yo, Adrian, Rocky called, he wants his face back.

SKYLER

I guess crime does pay.

[EP.7]

> **GUS**
> I hide in plain sight, same as you.

[EP.11]

> **GUS**
> You are a wealthy man now. And one
> must learn to be rich. To be poor, anyone
> can manage.

[EP.13]

> **WALT**
> Look, I saved your life, Jesse. Are you
> gonna save mine?

"It was you – all
along, it was YOU!
You son of a bitch."
– Hank Schrader

NAME: HENRY R. SCHRADER

AKA: HANK, AGENT SCHRADER

Hank Schrader, husband of Marie Schrader
(Skyler's sister) and brother-in-law to Walt,
also happens to be Agent Schrader in the
Albuquerque office of the United States Drug
Enforcement Agency. Hank is obsessed with
tracking down Heisenberg, the mysterious
figure behind the blue meth that is plaguing
his streets. Oblivious at first to Walt's double
life, Hank gets ever closer to uncovering his
secret. When he becomes wheelchair-bound
as a result of a shoot-out, Hank becomes
miserable and bored – until a particularly
intriguing murder case makes its way into
his hands and reignites his old obsession.

SEASON 4

[EP.1]

> **WALT**
> You kill me, you have nothing. You kill
> Jesse, you don't have me.

> **JESSE**
> We're all on the same page.
>
> **WALT**
> And what page is that?
>
> **JESSE**
> The one that says: "If I can't kill you, you'll
> sure as shit wish you were dead."

[EP.2]

> **MIKE**
> You won, Walter. You got the job. Do
> yourself a favor and learn to take "yes"
> for an answer.

[EP.3]

> **JESSE**
> For what it's worth, getting the shit kicked
> out of you . . . not to say you get used to it
> . . . but you do kind of get used to it.

[EP.4]

HANK

'W.W.' . . . I mean, who do you figure that is?
Woodrow Wilson? Willy Wonka? Walter White?

WALT

Heh. You got me.

[EP.5]

MIKE

You are not the guy. You're not capable of being
the guy. I had a guy but now I don't. You are not
the guy.

WALT

This genius of yours . . . maybe he's still out there.

[EP.6]

WALT

You clearly don't know who you're talking to
so let me clue you in. I am not in danger, Skyler.
I am the danger.

"Facing death changes
a person. It has to,
don't you think?"
– Marie Schrader

NAME: MARIE SCHRADER

(née Lambert)

Marie Schrader is Skyler's sister and wife to
DEA agent Hank Schrader. Marie and Skyler
seem to have a close relationship but both hide
big secrets from each other; Marie has a
problem with shoplifting and Skyler launders
drugs money. Marie has no children but
adores her nephew and little niece, stepping in
to look after them when the going gets tough
for Skyler and Walt. She works as a radiologic
technologist at Kleinman Radiology Center,
a medical scanning and X-ray office.

NAME: WALTER WHITE JR.

AKA: "FLYNN"

Born with cerebral palsy, Walt Jr. needs
crutches to help him get around and has
speech difficulties. He is a student at J. P.
Wynne High School, where his father taught
chemistry. He is a devoted son but becomes
anxious and angry when his life is disrupted
by the actions of his father. During this time
he chooses to be known as Flynn.

"The bad way to
remember you would
be the way you've
been this whole last
year. At least last
night you were...
real." – Walter Jr.

[EP.6]

> **WALT**
> A guy opens his door and gets shot, and you think
> that of me? No. I am the one who knocks.

> **SKYLER**
> Someone has to protect this family from the man
> who protects this family.

[EP.7]

> **WALT**
> Skyler, this is a simple division of labor. I bring
> in the money, you launder the money.

> **MIKE**
> All right, what's the order of the day?

> **JESSE**
> Eyes open, mouth shut.

[EP.12]

HANK
Just one man's humble opinion, that's all.
But I think Los Pollos Hermanos is a front for
the biggest meth distributor in the southwest.

[EP.13]

SAUL
You two want to stick your wangs in a hornet's
nest, it's a free country, but how come I get
sloppy seconds, huh?

GUS
What kind of man talks to the DEA? No man.
No man at all.

SKYLER
What happened?

WALT
I won.

"All right, $16,000 laundered at 75 cents on the dollar, minus my fee, which is 17%, comes out to $9,960. Congratulations, you've just left your family a second hand Subaru."
– Saul Goodman

NAME: SAUL GOODMAN

AKA: JIMMY MCGILL

Saul Goodman is an often inappropriate, but
surprisingly savvy ambulance-chasing attorney
who works for Walt and Jesse, providing
them with unconventional, but sage advice
regarding their criminal activities. He is well
known locally for his low-budget television
commercials and print advertisements, which
sell his services using the tagline, "Better
Call Saul!" When Saul first meets Walt, he
tells him that he is actually of Irish decent
and not Jewish, claiming that his real name
is McGill. Despite his shady appearance,
Saul is an excellent lawyer who always gets
the best deal for his clients due to his in-
depth knowledge of various legal loopholes.
The situation becomes precarious for Saul
as he continues to play both ends against
the middle, representing Walt and Jesse
even when their interests start to diverge.

SEASON 5a

[EP.1]

> **MIKE**
> You know how they say, "It's been a pleasure?"
> It hasn't.

> **WALT**
> We're done when I say we're done.

[EP.2]

> **MIKE**
> You are a time bomb, tick, tick, ticking, and I
> have no intention of being around for the boom.

[EP.3]

> **SKYLER**
> Shut up! Will you shut up?! Shut the hell up!
> Shut up! Shut up! Shut Up!

> **MIKE**
> Listen, Walter. Just because you shot Jesse
> James doesn't make you Jesse James.

[EP.4]

> **WALT**
> What are you waiting for?

> **SKYLER**
> For the cancer to come back.

[EP.5]

> **JESSE**
> Sounds like she's telling the truth to me.

> **MIKE**
> She has a gun to her head, kid. Everyone sounds like Meryl Streep with a gun to their head.

> **SKYLER**
> I'm not your wife. I'm your hostage.

[EP.6]

> **WALT**
> I'm in the empire business.

[EP.7]

> **WALT**
> Say my name.

> **DECLAN**
> You're Heisenberg.

> **WALT**
> You're goddamn right.

> **MIKE**
> Shut the fuck up . . . and let me die in peace.

[EP.8]

> **SKYLER**
> Walt . . . I want my kids back. I want my life back. Please tell me. How much is enough? How big does this pile have to be?

NAME: GUSTAVO FRING
AKA: GUS

Gustavo "Gus" Fring, a respectable local
businessman, owns several businesses
including a laundry and a popular regional
fast food chain, Los Pollos Hermanos. Despite
his friendly, unassuming outward appearance,
he's also secretly one of the biggest meth
distributors in the Southwest.

When Gus hired Walt and Jesse as his meth
cooks, his operation became a bit messier than
his hallmark professional reputation
demanded – and he didn't like that one bit.
Gus's relationship with Walt went downhill
fast after Walt killed two of his dealers in
order to protect Jesse. But this disagreement
paled into insignificance with the
encroachment of the Mexican cartel and the
skeletons that litter Gus's mysterious closet
soon began to rattle.

"What does a man do, Walter? A man provides for his family. And he does it even when he's not appreciated, or respected, or even loved. He simply bears up and he does it. Because he's a man."
– Gustavo Fring

SEASON 5b

[EP.9]

> ### WALTER
> Hello, Carol.

> ### SKYLER
> Have an A-1 day.

> ### HANK
> I don't know who you are... I don't even know who I'm talking to...
>
> ### WALT
> If that's true... If you don't know who I am, then... maybe your best course would be to tread lightly.

[EP.10]

> ### SKYLER
> Am I under arrest?

> ### SKYLER
> Hank. I think maybe I need a lawyer.

[EP.10]

SAUL

In case you need me? I'm thinking the probability
is high.

_____

HUELL

Mexico. All I'm sayin.

_____

WALT

Send him to Belize. I'll send you to Belize.

_____

MARIE

Who are you, Lone Wolf McQuade?

_____

[EP.11]

JESSE

Tell me one more time to calm down.

_____

SAUL

I'm gonna get a bag for the cash. Hey! Don't even
think about lighting up in here!

_____

SAUL

Well, then you *get* my complete lack of chill.

"I chose a half measure,
when I should have
gone all the way...
I'll never make that
mistake again. No more
half measures, Walter."
– Mike Ehrmantraut

NAME: MICHAEL EHRMANTRAUT

AKA: MIKE

Mike's past as a Philadelphia police officer
left him with a knack for fixing – or covering
up – unpleasant situations. Hit man, private
investigator and cleaner, Mike is a man of
many talents. Sometimes a guardian angel,
sometimes an agent of vengeance; it's hard
to know where you stand with him.

After Gus placed Jesse in Mike's care, he
grew to like him, but he never warmed to
Walt and was instrumental in turning Jesse
against him, leaving Walt fearful for his
own life. Mike's role as the middleman and
go-to guy became increasingly dangerous
and messy as new threats emerged.
Watching him spend time with his adored
granddaughter, Kaylee, it's hard to believe
that Mike is a cold-blooded killer.

WALT

You think we've come all this way just to let something like lung cancer take me down? Not a chance.

JESSE

Mister White. He's the devil. He's smarter than you. He's ... luckier than you. Whatever you think is supposed to happen, the exact reverse opposite is gonna happen.

HANK

The kid? Oh, you mean the junkie that's dribbling all over my guest bathroom floor.

[EP.13]

HANK

Nice poker face.

JESSE

Fire in the hole, bitch.

WALTER
The reaction has begun.

WALT
Pinkman. You still owe me.

WALTER
I built this. Me, me alone.
Nobody else.

WALTER
I've still got things left to do.

SAUL
You mind if I give you a nickel's
worth of advice?

WALTER
Elliott, if we're gonna go
that way, you'll need a
bigger knife.

WALTER
I did it for me. I liked it.
I was good at it. And I was
really... I was alive.

JESSE
Say the words. Say you want
this. Nothing happens till I
hear you say it.

WALTER
I want this.

JESSE
Then do it yourself.